"BECOME A LIFE BUILDER"

Six Essential Tools To Build Your Success Story.

BY

John M. Debnam

DISCLAIMER

TABLE OF CONTENT

DESCRIPTION

To become a successful life builder, one must go on a journey, define, plan, experiment, fail, examine, and make mistakes. In order to experience success, we must first establish what we are aiming to achieve.

This book discusses actual ideas that will allow you to construct a prosperous life. Knowing what financial literacy is, how to attain financial success, developing wealth and financial freedom, knowing the main character traits for wealth, getting wealthy / maintaining wealth. Read and implement to become a remarkable and successful life builder.

INTRODUCTION

Everyone has their own unique explanation of how the world works. As Investor Michael Batnick explains, "Some lessons have to be experienced before they can be understood." We are all victims, in different ways, of that fact. And what you have experienced is more interesting than what you learn. So all of us go through life experiences and a set of assumptions about how money works that vary drastically from one person to another. The person who grew up in poverty thinks about risk and reward in ways the kid of a wealthy man cannot grasp if he tried. What appears strange to you could make sense to someone else.

To become a successful life builder, one must go on a journey, define, plan, experiment, fail, examine, and make errors. To experience success, we must first establish what we are aiming to achieve. I describe success as living according to our values. (or self-worth) in our daily life.

This book discusses actual ideas that can allow you to construct a prosperous life. Knowing what financial literacy is, how to attain financial success, develop wealth and financial independence, and get wealthy /stay affluent. This book will aid you as you read and implement.

CHAPTER ONE

FINANCIAL LITERACY

Financial literacy is the capacity to understand and effectively utilize various financial abilities, including personal financial management, budgeting, and investing. When you are financially literate, you have the basis of a relationship with money, and it is a life path of learning. The earlier you start, the better off you will be, because knowledge is the key to success when it comes to money.

The phrase "financial literacy" refers to a multitude of critical financial abilities and ideas. Financially savvy people are often less prone to financial fraud. A good foundation of financial literacy may assist many life objectives, such as saving for college or retirement, handling debt wisely, and operating a company. Key parts of financial literacy include learning how to construct a budget, prepare for retirement, manage debt, and track personal spending. Financial literacy may be achieved via reading books, listening to podcasts, subscribing to financial material, or talking to a financial practitioner.

Understanding Financial Literacy.

Being financially illiterate can lead to different kinds of dangers, such as being more likely to accrue unsustainable debt loads, either by unnecessary spending, bad spending decisions, or a lack of long-term planning. This, in turn, can lead to poor credit, bankruptcy, accumulated debt, and other undesirable aftereffects.

Financial literacy can assist in protecting individuals from being victims of financial fraud, a sort of crime that is growing increasingly widespread.

Scope of Financial Literacy.

Although many abilities could come under the banner of financial literacy, prominent examples include household budgeting, knowing how to manage and pay off debts, and analyzing the tradeoffs between different credit and investment options. These abilities frequently involve at least a rudimentary grasp of important financial principles, such as compound interest and the time value of money.

Other goods, such as mortgages, student loans, health insurance, and self-directed investment accounts, have also expanded in prominence. This has made it even more vital for folks to learn how to utilize them appropriately.

Financial literacy may involve short-term financial strategy as well as long-term financial strategy, and which approach you follow will rely on various aspects, such as your age, time horizon, and risk tolerance. Financial literacy comprises recognizing how investment decisions made now may affect your tax bills in the future.

Why Financial Literacy Matters.
From day-to-day spending to long-term budget forecasts, financial literacy is vital for handling these elements. It is crucial to plan and save enough to provide appropriate income in retirement while avoiding high amounts of debt that can result in bankruptcy, defaults, and foreclosures.

Benefits of Financial Literacy.
Holistically, the purpose of financial literacy is to enable individuals to make wiser decisions. More precisely, financial literacy is vital for a variety of reasons.

- Financial literacy can prevent catastrophic mistakes: Floating rate loans may have to change interest rates each month, whereas typical individual retirement account (IRA) deposits can't be withdrawn until retirement. Seemingly benign financial actions may have long-term effects that cost individuals money or disrupt life goals. Financial literacy helps individuals avoid making catastrophic mistakes with their finances.

- Financial literacy prepares people for emergencies: Financial literacy themes such as saving or emergency preparedness help individuals be ready for the unpredictable. Though losing a job or having a significant unexpected bill are always financially damaging, an individual may lessen the blow by practicing their financial literacy in advance by being ready for emergencies.

- Financial knowledge can help individuals attain their goals: By better knowing how to budget and save money, individuals may build plans that set expectations, keep them accountable to their finances, and set a route for accomplishing unreachable goals. Though someone may not be able to afford a desire today, they can always establish a plan to better raise their odds of making it happen.

- Financial literacy instigates confidence: Imagine making a life-changing decision without all the knowledge you need to make the best decision. By being equipped with the necessary information about finances, individuals may approach big life choices with better confidence and assurance that they are less likely to be startled or unfortunately impacted by unanticipated consequences.

Strategies to Improve Financial Literacy Skills.
Developing financial literacy to enhance your finances entails studying and practicing several skills linked to budgeting, managing, and paying off debts, and understanding credit and investment products. The good news is that, no matter where you are in life and financially, it's never too late to start adopting healthy financial habits. Here are some practical strategies to consider.

- Create a budget: Track how much money you get each month versus how much you spend on an Excel sheet, on paper, or using a budgeting app. Your budget should incorporate income (paychecks, investments, alimony), fixed costs (rent/mortgage payments, utilities, loan payments), discretionary spending (nonessentials such as eating out, shopping, and vacation), and savings.

- Pay yourself first: To develop savings, this reverse budgeting technique entails establishing a savings goal, such as paying for higher education, deciding how much you want to contribute toward it each month, and setting that amount away before you divvy up the rest of your costs.

- Pay bills promptly: Stay on top of monthly invoices, ensuring that payments routinely arrive on time. Consider taking advantage of automatic debits from a bank account or bill-pay applications and sign up for payment reminders (by email, phone, or text)

- Manage debt: Use your budget to keep on top of debt by cutting expenditures and boosting repayment. Develop a debt reduction plan, like paying down the loan with the highest interest rate first. If your debt is considerable, contact lenders to renegotiate repayment, consolidate debts, or locate a debt counseling program.

- Invest in your future: If your workplace provides a 401(k) retirement savings plan, be sure to join up and contribute the maximum to earn the employer match. Consider starting an individual retirement account (IRA) and constructing a diverse investment portfolio comprising equities, fixed income, and commodities.

If required, get financial guidance from expert advisors to help you evaluate how much money you will need to retire comfortably and design methods to attain your objective.

Importance of Financial Literacy.

Being financially literate from an early age offers an individual the tools and resources they need to be financially reliable later in life. The lack of financial literacy can lead to several dangers, such as building unsustainable debt loads, either via bad spending decisions or a lack of long-term preparedness. This, in turn, can lead to poor credit, bankruptcy, house foreclosure, or other undesirable repercussions.

How to Become Financially Literate.

Becoming financially literate entails studying and applying many skills related to budgeting, managing and paying off debts, and understanding credit and investment products. Basic actions to enhance your finances include setting a budget, keeping track of costs, being careful about regular payments, being smart about saving money, frequently checking your credit report, and investing for your future.

The Principles of Financial Literacy.

There are five major concepts of financial literacy. Though alternative models may specify different important components, the main purpose of financial literacy is to educate individuals on how to earn, spend, save, borrow, and protect their money.

CHAPTER TWO

WAYS TO SAVE MONEY

There are general ways to save money and some tips when it comes to banking, credit and debt, entertainment, family and friends, food, health, home and transportation savings.

General Ways to Save

- An emergency fund is a must. Chances are you've already been told that you need an emergency fund somewhere in the ballpark of three to six months of your income. Yes! Overwhelming, right? I recommend starting with an emergency fund savings goal of just $500.

- Establish your budget. The best way to jumpstart establishing a budget is to realize your spending habits. On the first day of a new month, get a receipt for everything you purchase throughout the month. Stack the receipts into categories like restaurants, groceries, and personal care. At the end of the month you will be able to clearly see where your money is going. Additionally, your bank or credit union may have this as an online-banking feature. Seeing what you spend in total on food, shopping, etc. can be humbling!

- Budget with cash and envelopes. If you have trouble with overspending, try the envelope budget system where you use a set amount of cash for most spending. And once the cash is gone, it's gone.

- Save automatically. Setting up automatic savings is the easiest and most effective way to save, and it puts extra cash out of sight and out of mind. Automatic savings means you have a process in place to save at regular intervals, whether that's monthly, weekly, or daily.

Instruct your employer to direct a certain amount from your paycheck each pay period and transfer it to a retirement or savings account (or both). Traditionally, you can set this up using your employer's direct deposit, ask your HR representative for more details and set this up today.

- 'Start Small. Think Big,' with a short- term goal. The truth is, people save more successfully when they set a short-term goal. For instance, committing to saving $20 a week or a month for 6 months is much more attainable than setting a goal to save $500 a month for a year. Once you reach the short-term goal, you'll have created a habit of saving you can be proud of! You'll be able to keep going strong with a new goal.

- Start saving for your retirement as early as possible. Few people get rich through their wages alone. It's the miracle of compound interest, or earning interest on your interest over many years, that builds wealth. Because time is on their side, the youngest workers are in the best position to save for retirement.

Take full advantage of employer matches to your retirement plan. Often as an incentive, employers will match a certain amount of what you save in a retirement plan such as a 401(k). If you don't take full advantage of this match, you're leaving money on the table.

- Save your windfalls and tax refunds. Every time you receive a windfall, such a work bonus, inheritance, contest winnings, or tax refund, put a portion into your savings account.

- Save your coins - literally. Putting aside just 50¢ a day over a year will get you almost halfway to an emergency fund. Check with your bank or credit union, and research apps that offer programs that round your purchases up to the nearest dollar and put the difference into a separate savings account.

- Use the 24-Hour Rule. Avoid purchasing expensive or unnecessary items on impulse with a self-imposed 24-hour rule. For any non-essential item, wait 24 hours before purchasing. It's perfect for online shopping where your items can simply be added to your cart to purchase later.

- Calculate purchases by hours worked instead of cost. This mental math tactic really helps you to think like a saver. Take the amount of the item you want to purchase and divide it by your hourly wage. For example, if you're considering a $50 pair of shoes and you make $10 an hour, ask yourself if those shoes are worth working for five hours. Sometimes they are, sometimes they won't be.

- Unsubscribe. Avoid temptation by unsubscribing from marketing emails and texts from the stores where you spend the most money. By law, each marketing email is required to

have an unsubscribe link, usually at the bottom of the email or you can reply to any text with STOP, and that should opt you out of their list.

- Place a reminder on your card. Remind yourself to think through every purchase by covering your card with a savings prompt such as, "Have you met your savings goal for the month?" Write the message on a piece of masking tape or colorful washi tape on your card.

- Participate in a local Investment Development Account (or IDA) program. If your income is low, you may be eligible to participate in an IDA program where your savings are matched. In return for attending financial education sessions and planning to save for a home, education, or business, you typically receive at least $1 for every $1 you save, and sometimes much more. That means $25 saved each month could become several hundred dollars by the end of the year. Find an IDA program near you.

Banking, Credit, and Debt Saving Tips

- Use only the ATMs of your bank or credit union. Using the ATM of another financial institution once a week might seem like no big deal, but if it's costing you $3 for each withdrawal, that's more than $150 over the course of a year.

- Pay your bills on auto-pay. This ensures they are paid on time, in full to avoid late charges. As a bonus, some loan providers offer a small interest rate deduction if you enroll in auto-pay.

- Get free debt counseling. The most widely available help managing your debt is with a Consumer Credit Counseling Services (CCCS) counselor. CCCS' network of non-profit counselors can work with you confidentially and judgment-free to help you develop a budget, figure out your options, and negotiate with creditors to repay your debts. Best of all, the 45-90 minute counseling sessions are free of charge and come with no obligations.

Entertainment Saving Tips

Take advantage of your library. Libraries are gold-mines of free entertainment. They offer several entertainment options including classes, e-books, and audio-books. Some libraries even allow you to borrow things like tools and sewing machines!

Volunteer at festivals. Cultural festivals and events often offer free admission to event volunteers. Contact the organizers of your favorite event to ask about volunteer opportunities and benefits.

Family and Friends Saving Tips

- Create a family spending limit on gifts. Discuss placing spending limits on gifts within your family and/or a system where you only purchase one gift for one person over the holidays. Not only will it relieve financial stress for your family, but it allows you to focus on what really matters during special occasions and holidays.

- Plan gift-giving well in advance. To go alongside spending limits, give yourself time! You'll ensure that you're giving the most thoughtful gifts, which usually end up being not as expensive. Besides, it will also give you the opportunity to look for sales.

- It's never too soon to start saving for college. The last thing kids need is more "stuff." Consider asking for donations to the college fund if you have enough clothes, toys, and other needs for your little ones.

- Designate one day a week a "no spend day." Reserve one night a week for free family and friends fun. Cook at home, and plan out free activities such as game night, watching a movie, or going to the park.

Food Saving Tips

- Commit to eating out one fewer time each month. Save money without sacrificing your lifestyle. Take small steps to reduce your dining budget. Start off with reducing the amount you eat out by just once per month.

- Plan your meals in advance and stick to a list while grocery shopping. People who do food shopping with a list, and buy little else, spend much less money than those who decide what to buy when they get to the food market. The annual savings could easily be hundreds of dollars.

- 'I'll take some water, thank you.' It's standard in the restaurant industry to mark up the cost of alcohol by three to five times. An easy way to cut down on your restaurant spending without changing your habits too drastically is to skip the beverages, alcoholic and non-alcoholic.

- Save time and money by doubling the recipe. Next time you make a family favorite, double the recipe and freeze the leftovers for another day. That way you can get two meals out of one and use the ingredients more efficiently with less waste.

Health Saving Tips

- Don't skimp on preventive healthcare. Routine dental checkups, for example, help prevent fillings, root canals, and dental crowns - all of which are expensive and no fun.

- Go generic. Ask your physician if generic prescription drugs are a good option for you. Generic drugs can cost several hundred dollars less to purchase annually than brand-name drugs. And since physicians often don't know the costs you incur for a particular drug, you often have to ask.

- Comparison shop for prescription drugs. Don't just rely on the closest drugstore because the cost to you can vary significantly from pharmacy to pharmacy. Make sure to check out your local pharmacist, supermarkets, wholesale clubs, and mail-order pharmacies.

- Purchase store brand over-the-counter medications. Store brand medications often cost 20-40 percent less than nationally advertised brands, but are the exact same formula.

Home Saving Tips

- Comparison shop for homeowners insurance. Before renewing your existing homeowners insurance policy each year, check out the rates of competing companies.

- Audit your home energy use. Ask your local electric or gas utility for a free or low-cost home energy audit. The audit may reveal inexpensive ways to reduce home heating and cooling costs by hundreds of dollars a year. Keep in mind that a payback period of less than three years, or even five years, usually will save you lots of money in the long-term.

- Weatherproof your home. Caulk holes and cracks that let warm air escape in the winter and cold air escape in the summer. Your local hardware store has materials, and quite possibly useful advice, about inexpensively stopping unwanted heat or cooling loss.

- Keep the sun out. Keep your blinds or curtains closed during hot summer days. Blocking the sunlight really does help to keep your house cooler.

- Use less water. Install low-flow shower-heads and faucet aerators to reduce your water usage and water costs.

- Cut laundry detergent use in half. Many laundry detergents on the market sold today are highly concentrated. Be sure to use the smallest suggested amount. Making laundry detergent is said to be relatively cheap and easy, especially if you prefer to use greener, natural products.

Go natural. Speaking of making your laundry detergent, using everyday items you already have around your home to clean works for many. You'd be surprised what you can do with vinegar and lemon!

- Lower the temperature on your water heater to 120 degrees. For every 10 degree reduction in temperature, you can save up to 5 percent on water heating costs.

Transportation Saving Tips

- Comparison shop for auto insurance. Before renewing your existing auto insurance policy each year, check out the rates of competing companies.

- Check multiple sites for low airfares. Want to plan your dream vacation for cheap? Don't rely on a single airline search engine to show you all inexpensive fares. Some discount carriers do not allow their flights to be listed in these third-party searches, so you need to check their websites separately.

CHAPTER THREE

HOW TO ACHIEVE FINANCIAL SUCCESS

Learn to Invest, Investing is Crucial.
Many individuals feel "investor" is not a word that pertains to them. In truth, anybody with any retirement account is an investor. That's crucial to understand since many individuals working today will not receive a guaranteed pension, which means they need to save considerable sums of money to finance their retirement. For most of us, merely putting money in a savings account won't be enough. Investing is a crucial instrument for developing your money. Diversified products like target-date retirement plans and mutual funds make investing easier than ever.

Choose Carefully, Every decision has a cost, so be careful to analyze your options.
Too frequently, people make financial decisions without thinking through the repercussions. For example, a customer believes they must have a thing, doesn't have enough cash, and utilizes a credit card to make the purchase without thinking about how much it will cost to pay off the debt. Or a couple buys a property without fully comprehending the conditions of the mortgage loan. When you select between two things, you automatically give something up. A decision

to buy an expensive automobile is a decision not to spend that money to buy other products or services, make an additional payment on your mortgage, or put extra money in your children's college savings fund. Before making that sudden purchase, make sure you think about the cost of your choices.

Invest In Yourself.
Education and training is your investment in you. Education and training is an important investment in you and your family. Investing wisely in higher education is surely one of the best financial decisions you can make for yourself in life. More education means higher earnings for life. Studies show more education leads to bigger paychecks. So, the more you learn, the more you earn.

Plan Your Spending, Know the Difference Between Net and Gross.

First-time workers often experience shock after receiving their first check. Income taxes, social security, and Medicare are just some of the deductions on most workers' earnings. When joining the workforce, make sure to develop a spending plan that takes into account the fact that approximately one-third of your earnings will be deducted from your paycheck.

Put Yourself on a Budget.

Make a budget, and stick to it. Financial success refers not so much to earning money or how much you are paid as it does to making wise choices about how to make use of your money. In other words, a financially successful person is crucially concerned about his or her choices when it comes to spending money. A budget is important for you and your family. Budgeting helps you to better plan and control your family's spending. Planning enables you to extend your buying power. A budget doesn't have to be complicated. All it takes is writing down how much comes in every month, how much must go out for rent, bills, food, and other expenses, and how you want to use what's left over. Gaining knowledge of where your money goes is key to exercising control over your spending.

CHAPTER FOUR

THE MAIN CHARACTER TRAITS FOR WEALTH.

These are the main five character traits for wealth that the wealthy people possesses, it includes:-
1. Working Smart and Hard
2. High - Risk Tolerance
3. Patience
4. Resilience
5. Voracious Readers and Observers

Work Smart and Hard

Smart work and hard work are two different character traits for wealth. Many wealthy people use a mix of smart work and hard work to build their wealth over time. The ability to balance working smart and working hard is a valuable skill that can help you become a life builder, in other words, a wealthy person. In this book, I define working smart and working hard, explain the differences between the two and provide tips for working smart.

What is working smart?

Working smart is using your resources and tools to achieve the best potential outcomes within the allotted time. Someone who works smart might apply their knowledge and expertise in their field to meet a goal while using minimal energy.

When you work smart, you may be able to increase your productivity, achieve a better work-life balance and excel in your career or business.

What is working hard?

Working hard is using high amounts of physical and emotional effort to achieve the best potential outcomes. Someone who works hard might consistently put in long hours to meet a goal. Working hard could also involve working intensely to complete a lot of tasks in a short time frame.

Smart work Vs hard work

Here are some differences between smart work and hard work that may help you identify when to use which one or both at the same time in order to acquire wealth.

- Approach: Hard work involves a direct approach in which you complete most of the work yourself to meet a deadline. While, The approach for working smart usually means you find the most efficient way to meet deadlines, including sharing work or prioritizing tasks.

- Time commitment: Working hard is usually most useful when you have an upcoming deadline and need to complete many tasks. While, Since smart work may take a little more time or organize and prioritize tasks, it's often best if you have a slightly longer time frame.

- Flexibility: Since hard work usually takes a direct approach to finish duties, there's usually less flexibility in the way you can work. While, Working smart often focuses mainly on flexibility to find the best ways to complete work.

- Focus: The main focus for hard work is quantity, since you try to complete as many tasks as possible. While, When you work smart, you usually focus on both quality and quantity to ensure you produce the best possible outcome.

Why working smarter is a good idea

- Your time and energy aren't things you should waste. Working smarter values your energy and optimizes your time. It helps you spend less time burning your energy and more time saving it for other important things. Plus, it makes you a more efficient worker. You know what tasks need to be accomplished in what order and the best strategies to use to complete them.

- It makes time for more rest: When you work smart, you rest smart, too. It gives you more time for all sorts of types of rest. That might involve meditating, practicing mindfulness, or even taking a nap. Short naps have been found to strengthen your memory, improve your mood, and boost your creativity.

- Helps to reduce or recover from burnout: Burnout zaps your energy levels and harms your mental health. But working smarter enables you to be mindful of your energy to recover or reduce burnout. Working smarter shows you how to connect with your values, what's meaningful to you, and your goals.

- Improves your work-life balance: Rather than work longer hours and be consumed by your professional life, working smarter carves our time for your personal life. Working smarter is a great time management practice that allows for more balance in your life and hitting deadlines on schedule.

- Boosts your work motivation: After a few days of working smart, the difference will be hard to ignore. Your motivation will increase because you'll be more productive and feel positive about your work. You'll see what this new strategy is doing for you, motivating you to set new goals and continue your growth.

- Improve your communication skills: Strong communication skills go a long way, whether you're an independent contractor, an entrepreneur, or a CEO. Improving your communication skills won't just benefit you, either it saves everyone time, including yours. You pay more attention to clear and concise communication, which also helps your decision-making abilities.Start by actively listening to people and sticking to one topic at a time.

- Makes you schedule tasks based on your energy levels: Working smarter enables you to figure out when you're the most productive and energized to work. Forcing yourself to work when your brain is tired won't produce good work. It'll only make you dread your tasks even more. Wealthy people know when to draw the line.

If you work better in the morning, schedule the important tasks that demand a lot of energy. Working to your strengths and not against them will help you get more done and feel more motivated.

High-Risk Tolerance

Risk tolerance is the degree of risk that an investor is willing to endure given the volatility in the value of an investment. An important component in investing, risk tolerance often determines the type and amount of investments that an individual chooses. An investor's future earning capacity, and the presence of other assets such as a home, pension, Social Security, or an inheritance affect risk tolerance. An investor can take greater risk with investable assets when they have other, more stable sources of funds available. Additionally, investors with a larger portfolio may be more tolerant to risk, as the percentage of loss is much less in a larger portfolio when compared to a smaller portfolio.

Greater risk tolerance is often synonymous with investment in stocks, equity funds, and exchange-traded funds (ETFs), while lower risk tolerance is often associated with the purchase of bonds, bond funds, and income funds.

Understanding Risk Tolerance

All investments involve some degree of risk and knowing their risk tolerance level helps investors plan their entire portfolio, determining how they invest. Based on how much risk they can tolerate, investors are classified as aggressive, moderate, and conservative.

One factor that affects risk tolerance includes the time horizon for an investor. Having a financial goal with a long time horizon, an investor may have greater returns by carefully investing in higher-risk assets, such as stocks. Conversely, lower-risk cash investments may be appropriate for short-term financial goals.

Aggressive Risk Tolerance

An aggressive investor, or one with a high-risk tolerance, is willing to risk losing money to get potentially better results.[1] Aggressive investors tend to be market-savvy with an understanding of the volatility of securities and follow strategies for achieving higher than average returns.

Their investments emphasize capital appreciation rather than income or preserving their principal investment. This investor's asset allocation commonly includes stocks and little or no allocation to bonds or cash.

Moderate Risk Tolerance

Moderate investors want to grow their money without losing too much. Their goal is to weigh opportunities and risks and this investor's approach is sometimes described as a "balanced" strategy.

Commonly, moderate investors develop a portfolio that includes a mixture of stocks and bonds, perhaps as a 50/50 or 60/40 structure.

An Example of a 60/40 Portfolio Structure is a moderate risk-tolerant investor may choose to invest in a 60/40 structure which may include a 60% investment in stocks, 30% in bonds, and 10% in cash.

Conservative Risk Tolerance

Conservative investors are willing to accept little to no volatility in their investment portfolios. Retirees or those close to retirement age are often included in this category as they may be unwilling to risk a loss to their principal investment and have a short-term investment strategy.

A conservative investor targets vehicles that are guaranteed and highly liquid. Risk-averse individuals commonly opt for bank certificates of deposit (CDs), money markets, or U.S. Treasuries for income and preservation of capital.

Patience

A patient man is always richer than an impatient one, even if the patient man has less money. What do I mean by that statement? Well, riches and wealth can take other forms besides dollars and cents. In what sense is the patient man richer? The answer is actually very simple. A patient man is always richer than the impatient one because the patient man can always afford to wait. The patient man is never desperate. The patient man has time to spare, while the man in a hurry is always on the verge of bankruptcy as far as time is concerned.

In any situation you can think of, impatience is a source of weakness and fear, while patience represents substance and strength. And here's another reason why patience gives the person who has it an incalculable advantage over those who don't: It gives him deeper insight into himself and others, which is a mark of philosophical refinement. If you can only see the short term, if you think only in terms of the here and now, then you are stuck in one place. You can't judge distances. You live in a world that's flat and two-dimensional. In other words, the impatient person lacks all sense of perspective.

Perspective lets you measure your current plans against things that have already occurred and against your desires and aspirations for the future. Then and now, here and there, near and far, need and know, watch and wait—these are the dual optics that allow the patient man to see in stereo. The nearsighted person sees only the present; the fantasizer sees only an imaginary future and, more likely, trips over his mistakes trying to get there.

Patience enables you to see the big picture. It helps you to make the most of today while building a better tomorrow. For that reason, it's one of the most valuable equities of all, one that you should make every effort to acquire if you actually want to become a life builder . The payoff will be worth it.

Be Resilient

To accumulate wealth, especially generational wealth, you'll need to endure decades of ups and downs. Getting to the point where you are wealthy is seldom in a straight line pointing upwards. You'll need resilience to navigate financial setbacks, such as unexpected expenses, market downturns, or job loss.

Oxford defines resilience as the capacity to recover quickly from difficulties; toughness. If we do set some big goals it goes without saying we will encounter obstacles along the way. Resilience is the process of getting back up as quickly as we can when we do encounter failure. Having a strong mission statement will enable us to bounce back faster.

The key to developing our own resilience is analyzing every tough experience by considering how the setback can turn out to be a good thing, and what we can do to make that happen. Do this, and you will be on your way to building wealth in no time.

Resilience also makes it easy for millionaires (or those on track to be millionaires) to be socially indifferent. When combined with persistence, this helps people stick to their goals and avoid "lifestyle creep" – which is the tendency to spend more whenever a person earns more.

Resilience helps people avoid this pressure, including from friends and colleagues. Essentially, people who develop these qualities don't feel pressured to keep up with the Joneses' and instead they "avoid distractions and the 'shiny object syndrome' the general population suffers from because millionaires aren't focused on what might make them happy today; they're focused on their long-term wealth-building plan. Spending above your means, spending instead of saving for retirement, spending in anticipation of becoming wealthy makes you a slave to the paycheck, even with a stellar level of income.

Wealthy People are Voracious Readers & Observers

Majority, self made, wealthy people are heavy readers. You can throw any newspaper or magazine at them and they will at least flip the pages from start to end. Reading more and more only improves people's observation. People do not care about things that they don't know about. But people who read more, know something about anything. This is what makes readers so observant. Reading makes people observant. In turn, observant people has more chances of

becoming wealthy. Readers tend to pounce quicker on opportunities. Opportunities come and go in everyone's way. But non-readers tend to reject them in ignorance. As wealthy people are mostly well read and informed, they tend to identify opportunities better compared to common people who read much less. You wanted to become wealthy by buying this book, so start reading books on investments, stock analysis, having multiple streams of income, etc.

CHAPTER FIVE

BUILDING WEALTH AND FINANCIAL FREEDOM

Financial freedom means possessing the ability to live the life you want without being anxious about money. It means having sufficient savings and investments to support your lifestyle, without the need to work for a salary or paycheck. Achieving financial freedom is a dream for many people, but it can seem like an impossible goal. However, with the right mentality and plans, it is possible to build wealth and achieve financial freedom. Achieving financial freedom can bring many benefits, including reduced stress, more time to pursue your passions, and the ability to leave a legacy for future generations. In this book, I will provide you with 6 actionable tips to help you on your journey toward financial independence.

Set Financial Goals and Create a Budget.
The first step towards gaining financial independence is to set clear financial objectives and build a budget. You need to know what your money is meant for and where you want it to be. Set realistic and quantifiable financial objectives, such as paying off debt, investing for retirement, or buying a property.

Then develop a budget that corresponds with your goals and allows you to live within your means.

Start a Side Hustle or Freelance Business.
Starting a side hustle or freelancing company may give you extra income streams and help you create wealth. Identify your abilities and talents, then create methods to monetize them. You may start small, with services like tuition, pet-sitting, or web design, and build your business over time.

Create Multiple Streams of Income.
Creating numerous income sources might offer you more financial stability and help you attain financial independence sooner. Look for ways to make passive income, such as investing in rental homes or launching an internet company. Diversify your revenue streams to decrease risk

and boost your earning potential. Set Financial Goals and Create a Budget

Invest in Real Estate

Investing in real estate may be a great strategy to generate wealth and attain financial freedom. Look for homes with a strong potential for appreciation or rental income. Consider partnering with other investors or using real estate investment trusts (REITs) to diversify your portfolio.

Live Below Your Means

Living below your means, means spending less than you earn and avoiding unnecessary expenditure. This might help you save money and invest in your future. Cut off from non-essential costs, such as dining out or buying expensive gadgets, rather prioritize your savings and investment goals.

Seek Professional Advice and Guidance.

Seeking expert counsel and assistance can help you make better financial decisions and prevent costly mistakes. Consider engaging with financial consultants, accountants, or attorneys who can give professional insights and help you design a unique plan for attaining your financial goals.

A financial adviser can help you establish a complete strategy for your money and assets, taking into consideration your present status and future aspirations. They can also assist in tax preparation, retirement planning, and risk management. An accountant can help you manage your taxes and keep track of your financial records. They can also advise on budgeting and financial planning. A lawyer can help you with legal matters relating to your finances, such as estate planning, making a will, or setting up a trust.

Before selecting a professional to work with, make sure to do your research and select someone who is experienced, trustworthy, and has a good reputation. You should also investigate their costs and how they are rewarded, since some consultants may operate on a commission basis while others charge a fixed fee or hourly rate.

CHAPTER SIX

GETTING WEALTHY VERSUS STAYING WEALTHY

There are numerous ways to acquire affluence and there is one way to stay wealthy: via a combination of frugality and paranoia. Getting money and maintaining money are two separate things and demand entirely distinct attitudes and techniques.

Getting money means taking risks, being positive, and putting yourself out there.
Staying Wealthy demands humility, and fear that everything you have created might be taken away from you just as soon as possible.

You need to prevent ruin at all costs. Having a "survival mentality" involves three things:

- Aim to be financially unshakable: Be able to stick out swings in the market and make sure to stay in the business long enough for compounding to work its magic.

- The most crucial thing to plan for: The plan won't go according to plan. A smart strategy gives space for error. "The more you need certain components of a plan to be accurate, the more brittle your financial plan becomes.

- Be positive about the future yet neurotic about the hurdles to your accomplishment. There is a delicate line between growing affluent and staying that way. individuals who don't have "enough" prefer to take more chances, whereas individuals who have adopted more of a preservative attitude.

Getting Wealthy

Getting wealthy needs a certain degree of risk, but more than that, you need a strong mental fortitude. Your aim in the investment process is to be in the game for as long as feasible. No one trade or investment should be able to pull you out of the market completely. Whether you opt to buy mutual funds or individual equities should be completely dependent on your capacity to endure the storm. Getting wealthy is a game of patience and perseverance.

Staying Wealthy

Wealth preservation is another story. This happens at the time in your life when you believe you have enough. Enough in the sense that extra money won't damage the lifestyle you have chosen.

CONCLUSION

Financial literacy is the understanding of how to make wise decisions with money. This includes setting a budget, knowing how much to save, determining advantageous loan conditions, comprehending the effects of credit, and identifying different vehicles utilized for retirement. These abilities help individuals make wiser judgments and act more responsibly with their finances.

If you are a younger individual now, retirement to you may seem years away. While it is a way in the future, it is also one of the finest objectives to start saving for, because the sooner you start, the more you'll have compounded down the line.

As a life builder, there are many ways to save money when it comes to banking, credit and debit, health, food, family and friends etc. One needs to accumulate wealth first and stay wealthy before spending unnecessarily. You have to spend wisely.

You, as a life builder, need these five main character traits to build your wealth because it will help you acquire wealth and maintain it.

Achieving financial freedom is not simple, but it is doable with the correct mentality, techniques, and actions. By following the 6 practical strategies I have offered in this book, you may start generating money and moving toward financial freedom. Remember to set clear goals, develop a budget, live below your means, invest consistently, and seek expert counsel when needed. Risk makes the most important distinction in either acquiring or remaining affluent. So be sure to keep this in mind while determining your goals in the investment industry.

Take the first step towards being a life builder by applying one of these recommendations now. Start small and develop momentum over time. At the end of the day, remember that you're growing, and that's something to be proud of. You can do it!